SEALS
OF THE ANTARCTIC

SARA SWAN MILLER

PowerKiDS
press™
New York

Published in 2009 by The Rosen Publishing Group, Inc.
29 East 21st Street, New York, NY 10010

First Edition

Editor: Amelie von Zumbusch
Book Design: Kate Laczynski
Photo Researcher: Jessica Gerweck

Photo Credits: Cover, back cover, pp. 1, 16, 20 Shutterstock.com; back cover (walruses) © Getty Images; back cover (caribou) © www.istockphoto.com/Paul Loewen; back cover (emperor penguins) © www.istockphoto.com/ Bernard Breton; back cover (polar bears) © www.istockphoto.com/Michel de Nijs; back cover (whales), p. 4 © Yva Momatiuk & John Eastcott/Getty Images; pp. 6, 18 © Paul Nicklen/Getty Images; p. 8 © Doug Allan/Getty Images; p. 10 © Joseph Van Os/Getty Images; p. 12 © Hiroya Minakuchi/Getty Images; p. 14 © Dr. Carleton Ray/Photo Researchers, Inc.

Library of Congress Cataloging-in-Publication Data

Miller, Sara Swan.
  Seals of the Antarctic / Sara Swan Miller. — 1st ed.
     p. cm. — (Brrr! Polar animals)
  Includes index.
  ISBN 978-1-4358-2745-5 (library binding) — ISBN 978-1-4358-3149-0 (pbk.)
ISBN 978-1-4358-3155-1 (6-pack)
  1. Seals (Animals)—Antarctica—Juvenile literature. I. Title.
  QL737.P64M55 2009
  599.7909989—dc22
                              2008030607

Manufactured in the United States of America

CONTENTS

Crabeater seals are the most common kind of Antarctic seal. However, people do not know much about them because they spend much of their time below the ice.

WHAT ARE SEALS?

Seals are **mammals** that spend most of their time swimming and diving in the ocean. There are two types of seals, eared seals and earless seals. The eared seals, also called fur seals, have earflaps on the sides of their heads. Earless seals, also called true seals, have only small holes. Both types of seals have very good hearing.

There are nineteen **species** of seals living in oceans around the world. Four of these species live in the waters off Antarctica, or the land around the South Pole. These are crabeater seals, Ross seals, Weddell seals, and leopard seals. All Antarctic seals are true seals.

Seals breathe through their nostrils, or the holes in their noses. A seal's nostrils are generally closed. Unlike most other mammals, seals must remember to breathe.

6

LOOKING AT SEALS

Seals have long, smooth bodies that help make them good swimmers. Different species of seals come in different sizes. The smallest species is only 4 feet (1 m) long. The longest seals are 20 feet (6 m) long. The seals of Antarctica are medium-sized seals. They are generally between 6 and 12 feet (2–4 m) long.

Instead of arms and legs, seals have **flippers**, which act like paddles. Antarctic seals hold their front flippers next to their bodies and move their back flippers from side to side to swim. Because seals are mammals, they need to come up to the **surface** to breathe.

Weddell seals, such as these two, have very good eyesight under water.
This helps them find food in the dark waters under the Antarctic ice.

STAYING WARM IN COLD WATERS

The Antarctic waters are very cold. Seals stay warm because they have a thick **layer** of fat, called blubber. Blubber acts sort of like a diver's wet suit, keeping the warmth in and the cold out. Blubber also helps seals swim smoothly under water. Seals are wonderful swimmers. Some Antarctic seals can dive as deep as 2,000 feet (600 m) down.

These seals may stay out at sea for weeks at a time. Some can hold their breath for over an hour! Antarctic seals have a harder time on land, though. They have to crawl along on their stomachs.

Mother seals generally have only one baby at a time. This lets the mother give her pup a lot of attention.

SEAL PUPS

Seals spend most of their time in the water. At **breeding** time, though, seals go up on land. Some types of seals pair off to breed. Other kinds of seals gather in big groups at breeding time. Then, males try to gather groups of females with which to breed. Males guard these groups from other males.

Nearly a year after its parents have **mated**, a pup is born. The pup is born on the ice, but it soon learns to swim. The mother's milk is very rich in fat. This helps the pup grow quickly. Antarctic seal pups nurse for two to six weeks. Then, they are on their own.

Crabeater seals eat a lot of krill. The seals can eat about 20 to 25 times their own weight every year.

HUNGRY CRABEATER SEALS

Crabeater seals are the most common kind of Antarctic seals. You might think crabeater seals eat a lot of crabs. However, these seals eat mostly krill. Krill are tiny creatures that look a lot like shrimp. Huge numbers of krill live in the Antarctic's cold ocean waters. Crabeater seals have special rounded teeth that act like a **sieve**. The seals take in a mouthful of krill and seawater and then push the water back out through their teeth.

In the spring, crabeater seals form small families. The families have a father, a mother, and one pup. The father guards the family.

Ross seals are named after the British navy officer James Clark Ross. Ross discovered the seals in 1840.

HARD-TO-FIND ROSS SEALS

There are fewer Ross seals than any other kind of Antarctic seal. Ross seals live mostly alone, and they are hard to get to know. Unlike many other seals, Ross seals have no spots. Instead, they have **streaks** down the sides of their necks. Sometimes the streaks look like a mask.

Ross seals are deep divers. Like other seals, they close their **nostrils** before they dive. Ross seals have extra large eyes that help them spot their **prey** in the dark waters. Their favorite food is **squid**. The seals chase squid down and snap them up with their sharp teeth. Ross seals also eat fish and krill.

Weddell seals have fairly small heads, light stomachs, and dappled, or spotted, backs.

LOUD WEDDELL SEALS

Weddell seals spend much of their time swimming under the Antarctic's fast ice. Fast ice is sea ice that touches land. Fast ice stays in one place and does not float around, as sea ice sometimes does. Weddell seals use their very long, strong teeth to chew breathing holes in the ice. They even mate under the ice. These seals are very loud. They make many different sounds to communicate, or speak, with each other. You can even hear their calls through the ice!

Weddell seals eat mostly fish and squid. They can creep up very close to a fish. Then, they snap up big chunks of fish without even chewing.

Leopard seals are strong, fast hunters. They can swim as fast as 25 miles per hour (40 km/h) while chasing their food.

BIG, SCARY LEOPARD SEALS

Can you guess how leopard seals got their name? Their spotted coats look a bit like a leopard's coat. These seals are like leopards in another way, too. Leopard seals are big, strong hunters. They have huge mouths, very strong **jaws**, and very sharp teeth. A leopard seal will eat almost anything smaller than itself.

One of these seals' favorite foods is penguins. Leopard seals wait underwater, near the edge of the ice, for penguins to jump into the water. Then, the seals catch them. Leopard seals will also swim up under seabirds resting on the water's surface and catch them.

Killer whales are also called orcas. These whales often hunt in groups. Around 160,000 killer whales live in the Antarctic.

WHO HUNTS SEALS?

Leopard seals can be a danger to other Antarctic seals. Crabeater seals are one of a leopard seal's favorite foods. Leopard seals also attack Ross seals and Weddell seals. Antarctic seals have to watch out for killer whales, too. Even leopard seals have to fear these large, hungry whales. It does no good to fight back. Killer whales are too big. The best way for a seal to stay safe from a killer whale is to swim away as fast as it can.

In the past, people were also a danger to Antarctic seals. People once hunted these seals for money. They sold the seals' skins, blubber, and meat.

KEEPING SEALS SAFE

Today, many countries and groups have signed an agreement to keep Antarctic seals safe. This agreement, called the Convention for the Conservation of Antarctic Seals, sets rules about seal hunting. Hunting seals is almost never allowed in the Antarctic anymore. It is also against the law to spray **pesticides** or dump garbage, or trash, there. Mining and drilling for oil in the Antarctic are not allowed, either, at least until 2041.

Thanks to these laws and rules, Antarctic seals seem to be doing well. Today, there are about 15 million crabeater seals and between 200,000 and 800,000 of each of the other three species!

GLOSSARY

breeding (BREED-ing) Having to do with making babies.

flippers (FLIH-perz) Wide, flat body parts that help animals swim.

jaws (JAHZ) The bones in the top and bottom of the mouth.

layer (LAY-er) One thickness of something.

mammals (MA-mulz) Warm-blooded animals that have backbones and hair, breathe air, and feed milk to their young.

mated (MAYT-ed) Came together to make babies.

nostrils (NOS-trulz) The openings of the nose.

pesticides (PES-tuh-sydz) Poisons used to kill pests.

prey (PRAY) Animals that are hunted by another animal for food.

sieve (SIV) Something that traps the bigger objects in a mix of things.

species (SPEE-sheez) One kind of living thing. All people are one species.

squid (SKWID) An animal with 10 legs that lives in the ocean.

streaks (STREEKS) Long, often messy, marks.

surface (SER-fes) The outside of anything.

INDEX

WEB SITES

Due to the changing nature of Internet links, PowerKids Press has developed an online list of Web sites related to the subject of this book. This site is updated regularly. Please use this link to access the list:
www.powerkidslinks.com/brrr/seal/